The Pequots

Shirlee P. Newman

Franklin Watts
A Division of Grolier Publishing
New York • London • Hong Kong • Sydney
Danbury, Connecticut

To Haley, with thanks to Paula and Mark
for introducing me to the Pequots.

Note to readers: Definitions for words in **bold** can be found in the Glossary at the back of this book.

Photographs ©: American Museum of Natural History: 38; Archive Photos: 30; Bridgeman Art Library International Ltd., London/New York: 31 (BL11806/The Crusher Squeezes Juice from the Cane, Antigua, by W. Clark, British Library, London, UK.), 32 (CH19669/Group of Indians on a River Bank, 1854, watercolour on paper by Friedrick Kurz/Christies's Images, London, UK); Corbis-Bettmann: 11, 40, 43, 44 (UPI), 21, 39; Liaison Agency, Inc.: 13 (Gifford), 4, 7, 16, 45 (Paul E. Johnson), 50 (D. Kampfner); Marilyn "Angel" Wynn: 3 bottom, 9 right, 12 bottom, 19 bottom; New England Stock Photo: 12 top, 52 (Michael Giannaccio), 36 (Brendon James), 46 (Lou Palmieri); North Wind Picture Archives: 9 left (N. Carter), 3 top, 22, 23, 25, 28; Peter Arnold Inc.: 14 bottom, 51 (John Cancalosi); Photo Researchers: 8 bottom (J. L. Lepore); Reinhard Brucker: 8 top, 10 top, 14, 18, 19 top, 20; Stock Montage, Inc.: 10 bottom, 26; Tony Stone Images: 49 (Rob Boudreau), 27 (Dave Schietelbein); Visuals Unlimited: 37 (Tom Ulrich).

Cover illustration by Gary Overacre, interpreted from a photograph by © Marilyn "Angel" Wynn

Map by XNR Productions Inc.

Visit Franklin Watts on the Internet at:
http://publishing.grolier.com

Library of Congress Cataloging-in-Publication Data

Newman, Shirlee P.
  The Pequots / Shirlee P. Newman
      p.   cm.— (Watts Library)
  Includes bibliographical references and index.
  ISBN:0-531-20327-1 (lib. bdg.) 0-531-16482-9 (pbk.)
  1. Pequot Indians—History—Juvenile literature. 2. Pequot Indians—Social life and customs—Juvenile literature. I. Title. II. Series.
E99.P53N48   2000
974'.00497—dc21   99-13702
                                                                         CIP

©2000 Franklin Watts, A Division of Grolier Publishing

Contents

The Pequot creation
story is set on an
ancient, sandy shore.

The Pequots' Foremothers

"Picture the beach on a hot summer day," a Pequot mother says when she tells her children the mythical story about how their tribe began. "The sun was high, the tide was low, and the berries at the edge of the shore were ripe. But no children played in the sand. No women picked the berries. No men dug clams at the edge of the water.

"Suddenly the bushes parted and two young women stepped onto the beach. Their long, dark hair streamed out behind them as they ran across the warm, dry sand. They shouted and laughed as they leaped into the sea and splashed each other with cool white foam.

"Then the days grew shorter. Gentle breezes became gusty winds and snow fell. After a while, the days grew longer. The sun rose higher. The snow melted. And both of the young women had babies. One of them had a boy, the other had a girl. Those babies grew up and had babies of their own. And that's how our tribe began. All the other Pequot people descended from them."

Opposite: The Connecticut River winds through Pequot land.

Chapter One

People of All Seasons

Pequots have lived in what is now Connecticut for thousands of years. Smaller tribes, such as the Montauketts, Western Niantics, and Mohegans lived nearby. The Narragansetts and the Eastern Niantics lived in what is now Rhode Island.

Food, Clothing, and Shelter

Dense forests provided wood for Pequots' homes. Their food came from the lakes, ponds, and rivers, and from the

Hunting arrows were used for spearing fish and game.

Valuable Spots

Native Americans made purple beads called **wampum** from the purple spots on quahogs' hard shells. They used wampum to decorate belts, necklaces, and they recorded events by arranging the beads in designs.

Long Island Sound, the arm of the Atlantic Ocean that separates Connecticut from Long Island. Pequots speared whales from dugout canoes, hunted **cormorants** and other water birds with bows and arrows. They caught turtles, fish, and lobsters in nets and traps, or with hooks and lines. Men, women, and children dug up scallops, oysters, sea snails, mussels, clams, and **quahogs,** or large clams, at the water's edge.

In hunting season, Pequot men hunted or trapped deer, bear, squirrel, geese, and wild turkey. They used deerskins to make their clothing. Pequot women soaked the deerskins in water and oil, then scraped off the flesh and fat and removed the hair. Then they stretched the skins on wooden frames and tanned them over a smoky fire. Finally, they made them into clothing, using bone needles and tough, threadlike animal tissue. Pequot men wore **breechcloths** that hung from the waist. Women wore skirts. In winter they both added shirts. Boys and girls dressed like the adults.

In gathering season, women and children collected wild berries, grapes, nuts, and edible roots. They boiled and roasted the roots and nuts, and stored them for winter.

This deer hide has been partially scraped.

Soup Thickener

Boiled acorns were ground, using a mortar and pestle, into a fine powder to thicken soup and stew.

In planting season, Pequot men burned down trees, weeds, underbrush, and tall grasses to clear the land. They **tilled** the soil with hoes made of sharpened stones or large clamshells attached to sticks. Men, women, and children planted and harvested corn, beans, squash, tobacco, and Jerusalem artichoke—a sunflower with a thick underground root tuber that was used as a vegetable.

Village Life

Most of the Pequots lived in small villages of about twenty homes, called **wigwams.** In summer, their homes were open to the cool ocean breezes. In winter, they were closed in and heated by a central fire. The Pequots built their wigwams by driving flexible poles into the ground. They bent the poles over until they met, fastened them together, and covered them with long strips of bark. Homes for one or two families were usually round. Their dirt floors were covered with woven mats. Larger houses, called longhouses, were big enough for fifty people. When the Pequots moved to the

Birch bark was used to build wigwams, as well as canoes.

Each longhouse was home to several families.

coast or to their hunting grounds, they left the frames and took along the rolled-up mats.

Each village had a **sachem**—a leader, or chief, who was in charge of dividing up the food and distributing it to the poor. Sachems also divided up the land among the families and were responsible for protecting tribal territory. They decided important matters in council with their **sagamores,** or assistants, and with villagers who had special knowledge or talent.

The Pequots also relied on **shamans**, or religious leaders, to tell them the best time to plant, hunt, or harvest. They believed that shamans were in touch with the spirits who ruled the world. These included the gods of the harvest and the hunt, as well as the gods of rain, thunder, and lightning. A special god looked after women. Another god took care of children.

Prince Leaping Deer offers prayers at Lantern Hill, the scene of many Pequot powwows.

Celebrations

The people of many villages gathered together to pray or give thanks for a successful hunt or a good harvest. The most important celebration of the year was Schemitzun, the Feast of the Green Corn and Dance, which took place when the first ears of corn ripened. Schemitzun was an opportunity for giving, sharing, or giving back. The feast lasted for three days, but preparing for it took weeks. Wigwams were built to shelter guests, and food was prepared to feed them. Pequot women cooked meat and seafood, and ground up corn to make **porridge**, bread, pudding, and fried cakes.

Gifts were exchanged when guests arrived. The people played games and told stories, but the main event was the dancing. Whole families joined the traditional dance circle. Babies in their parents' arms rocked back and forth to the beat of the drums. Small children and elders held hands and danced together. Shamans, wearing a variety of masks, sang and danced as they tossed wam-

Dancing gave tribal gatherings like Schemitzun a festive atmosphere.

A shaman sings a sacred song in praise of the moon.

pum, furs, and food into the fire as sacrifices to the gods.

During the festival, young Pequot men played a noisy, exciting ball game that the English called stickball and the French called *lacrosse*. It was a rough game and players often got hurt. Players used sticks with woven nets or leather loops at one end to catch the ball. They struck each other's sticks, kicked and wrestled, and carried or threw the ball through the goalposts.

Hiding the Bones was a favorite game for both children and adults. Two teams sat opposite each other. To begin with, the hiding team beat drums, rattled poles, sang, made faces, and did tricks to divert the guessing team's attention. Meanwhile, a member of the hiding team hid the bones in unlikely places such as a team member's clothing, behind someone's back, or under someone's foot.

Many American Indian tribes played lacrosse.

Laughter, singing, and clacking of poles often continued long after the children had settled down by the fire to listen to elders' stories. One story tells how Tiny Weak Woman escaped from Big Mean Man by tossing eggs from her canoe as he chased her in his canoe. The churning water beat up the

The Snow Snake Game

The Pequots played games throughout the year. In winter, they played the Snow Snake Game. First, they made a long, straight ditch by dragging a log through the snow. Each player had a "snake," a polished pole with one end carved to look like a snake's head. The players tried to throw their "snakes" as far as possible along the ditch. To make them travel farther, the players dipped their "snakes" in water and left them outside to freeze.

Native American children today still enjoy the ancestors' stories.

eggs till they became so thick and gooey that Big Mean Man's canoe got stuck.

Another story tells of a powerful god who bragged that he could frighten anyone. The god was proved wrong when a baby he tried to frighten wasn't scared at all. The baby didn't even cry. Instead, he said "Meconchatoon," a Pequot word that means "I am thirsty," and "meen," which means "milk."

These and other tales have been favorites of Pequot children and those of other Algonquian-speaking people down through the ages.

Pequot Language

The following Pequot words and phrases were translated by Reverend James Noyes of Stonington, Connecticut, in the 1600s.

a basket	*minnoot*	a day	*cheesnesod*
a bead	*mazawmpe*	milk	*meen*
a bed	*cauhcouemuk*	eat	*mitth*
greetings	*ashmeconca*	thanks	*tabut hough*
chair	*aughpubmuck*	fish	*squuttah*
I am hungry	*nuschiantum*	water	*nipp*
a cat	*popse*	head	*chuanunk*
I	*ne*	house	*weigoh*
I cannot	*matchog*	great	*mshiow*
leg	*acaunt*	yes	*nun*

Abundant farmland and wildlife are found along the Connecticut River.

Chapter Two

War

In 1614, Adriaen Block, a Dutch explorer, sailed into Long Island Sound and up the Connecticut River. He wrote in his journal about the "Pequatoos" who lived in nearby villages. The "Pequatoos" were the Pequots. Impressed with the region's wildlife and other natural resources, Block claimed the land for the Netherlands, and in 1633, Dutch traders established a trading post 50 miles (80 kilometers) north of Long Island Sound, where the city of Hartford now stands.

In the meantime, English colonists from Plymouth and Massachusetts Bay colonies had been exploring the area by

This museum exhibit recreates a typical trading post.

boat. They, too, were impressed with the region's natural resources. That same year they established a trading post on the Connecticut River and settled at what are now Windsor, Hartford, and Wethersfield. The English also built Fort Saybrook, where the Connecticut River runs into Long Island Sound.

The Pilgrims

A pilgrim is a person who travels far to search for religious freedom. The people in Plymouth Colony became known as the Pilgrims because they left the Church of England in 1607 and moved to the Netherlands, to be able to worship as they pleased. In 1620, they sailed to America on the ship *Mayflower*.

Explorers from Europe brought many things with them—including deadly diseases to which Native Americans were not **immune.** Thousands of them died, including the entire population of many Pequot villages. Only about 3,000 Pequots survived. These remaining Pequots lived in twenty-six villages. They expanded their territory in several directions, and hunted and planted on islands in Long Island Sound.

The English colonists wrote back to England that the Pequots were warlike people. It is true that the Pequots were the largest and most

Ancient stone tools (above) and rock etchings (below) provide clues about Pequot lifestyle and beliefs.

Stylish Hats

In Europe at that time, a large beaver hat was a symbol of a man's wealth.

powerful tribe in southern Connecticut, but some historians feel they were not as warlike as the colonists were. The historians believe that much of what the colonists wrote was **racist**, prejudiced, and intended to impress the authorities back in England.

English colonists also wrote that the Pequots had come to the region from the Hudson River Valley in New York State shortly before the colonists arrived. However, archaeologists, scientists who study ancient remains, have recently found proof that the Pequots had lived in what is now Connecticut for thousands of years. The colonists also said that the Pequots were aimless wanderers. The colonists did not mention that Pequots "wandered" from place to place to find food in changing seasons. They moved to the coast in summer to eat fish and they moved inland in fall to gather roots and berries, to farm, and to hunt.

Fur-bearing animals were plentiful in the Connecticut River Valley. The beaver's soft, glossy undercoat was especially good for clothing.

A substance in beaver glands was also used in perfume. This was in great demand in Europe, because Europeans seldom bathed. They sprayed themselves with perfume instead. With such huge profits to be made, English and Dutch traders competed for trade with the Indians.

Eager Traders

The Pequots had always traded with other tribes, and they gladly traded with the Europeans for metal knives, ax heads, farming tools, cloth, and other things manufactured in Europe.

Wampum is presented to the Chief.

After a while, many Pequots felt they couldn't get along without these things. Unfortunately, they became involved in the competition between English and Dutch traders. This led to a war in 1637 that killed or enslaved hundreds of Indians and almost wiped out the Pequot tribe forever.

War against the Pequots

Relations between Dutch traders and the Pequots were friendly until a Dutch trader captured Tatobom, a Pequot sachem. The Dutch held Tatobom for **ransom**. They demanded to be paid in wampum, which traders used as money to buy furs from other tribes. The Pequots paid the ransom, but the trader killed Tatobom anyway. The Pequots then attacked the Dutch trading post. In the fighting, the Pequots also killed some Narragansetts who were trading there. As a result, the Dutch stopped trading with the Pequots, and the Narragansetts prepared for war.

To try to keep peace and resume trade with Europeans, the Pequots sent a few men to the colonial city of Boston, Massachusetts. They asked the colonial authorities to send

Pequot messengers with Roger Williams, founder of Rhode Island and friend to the Indians, during the Pequot War

another English trader to Connecticut. The English did send another trader, but he was killed on his boat off the shore of Block Island. The Eastern Niantics and Narragansetts lived closest to the island, but the English blamed the Pequots for the trader's death. They demanded that the Pequots turn over the killers and pay a large fine of wampum and furs. The English also demanded that the Pequots bring them some children to hold as hostage to ensure future peace.

The Pequots gave the English wampum and furs, but refused to turn over children or men. Then English soldiers, claiming to search for the trader's killers, burned Pequot homes and crops. The soldiers were also responsible for the death of a Pequot. After this happened, the Pequots stationed

Settlers at Fort Saybrook meet at the shore of the Connecticut River.

Wealth and Power

The Narragansetts had escaped the worst epidemics of European diseases that swept the area in the early 1600s. They grew rich by trading wampum and furs with the English, and they remained strong for the rest of the century.

some of their men near Fort Saybrook and killed two English soldiers who ventured outside the fort.

In April 1637, English settlers near Wethersfield had driven members of a small group of Indians under Pequot protection from their homes. The Pequots then killed some Englishmen near there, and captured two teen-aged girls.

A month later, Dutch traders sought permission from the English at Fort Saybrook to sail up the Connecticut River. They captured seven Pequots and threatened to drown them if the girls were not released. The prisoners on both sides were exchanged, and the girls were returned to their families, but death and devastation lay ahead.

The Turning Point

The sky was still dark on that spring day in 1637. The sun had not yet risen and all was quiet in the Pequot village near what is now Mystic, Connecticut. Most of the young men were away hunting, fishing, or at the Pequot fort located 5 miles (8 km) east. Women, children, and elderly men were sleeping as English soldiers and their Narragansett, Mohegan, and Eastern Niantic allies silently surrounded the village. Suddenly, shots rang out. Soldiers had crashed through the gates and killed seven Pequots.

"We must burn them," Captain John Mason, the English commander shouted as the sleepy Pequot people sprang up from their mats and ran about. Torches were tossed at some of their homes, and ocean breezes fanned the flames. They sput-

English Hero

The English praised John Mason. A statue of him stands in West Mystic, Connecticut, where a Pequot village once stood.

Mason's troops massacred the Pequots and destroyed their village.

The war against the Pequots continued over many years.

tered and sparked until all eighty homes caught fire. Girls and boys, mothers, grandmothers, and grandfathers burned to death as the village turned to ashes.

The soldiers killed the Pequots who tried to escape, and more than four hundred people died in less than an hour. No one knows how many were captured. Sassacus, the Pequot sachem, and some of his followers escaped and sought refuge with the Mohawks, a tribe in New York State. The Mohawks killed the Pequots, sent the English their heads, and collected the **bounty.**

English soldiers continued to search out and kill or capture any Pequots they could find. The soldiers killed thirty Pequot men and captured a hundred starving women and children hiding in a swamp. Great masses of rhododendrons with yellow centers bloomed in that swamp every year. According to legend, Puttaquapouk, the Pequot leader, said the flowers would never be the same. Since then, they have bloomed with deep red centers that seem to drip with Pequot blood.

The blood-red rhododendron has become a symbol of the Pequots' fate.

Slavery awaited those Pequots who survived the war.

Chapter Three

Slavery

Some of the Pequots captured during the war were sold to Connecticut or Massachusetts colonists to work in homes and on farms. Governor John Winthrop of Massachusetts sent others farther away. Some teen-aged Pequots went to Bermuda, and some ended up in the West Indies.

In Bermuda

Bermuda was an English colony made up of three hundred small islands in the Atlantic Ocean—more than 800 miles (1,288 km) away from the Pequots' homeland. They were crowded together on a small ship and taken south on the rough waters of the Atlantic. Some died on the way.

According to Bermudan records, more than a hundred Pequots arrived in Bermuda in 1640. A sea captain who lived on St. David's, one of the islands in the Bermuda chain, bought some of them. Other Pequots were sold on other Bermuda islands or shipped to the West Indies where prices for slaves were higher. They were sold for their lifetime or ninety-nine years.

Some Pequots on Bermuda tried to escape. They were often found hiding in caves and returned to their owners. Escape by boat was almost impossible because Bermuda is 700 miles (1,126 km) away from any other island and surrounded by dangerous reefs. Still, in 1641, Governor John Winthrop, Jr., of Connecticut wrote in his journal that three Indian boys had landed on a Long Island beach after more than two months at sea. They may have been Pequots.

Working conditions for slaves in Bermuda were usually better than those in the West Indies. Girls in Bermuda probably worked in English homes. Boys worked on sugar plantations, or on boats as fishermen, crewmen, or whalers. Some worked on ships that crossed the Atlantic and many tried to gain their freedom by escaping from the ship when it landed in England. Most were caught and forced to return to the ship.

John Winthrop (1606–1676), Governor of Connecticut

A sugarcane processing plant

In the West Indies

Most slaves in the West Indies worked on sugar plantations. During the rainy season, they dug holes and planted, fertilized, and weeded sugarcane. After the rainy season, they spent their days cutting cane under a blistering hot sun. Then they had to turn the rollers on the sugar mill and stir the hot, steaming cane over huge open pots.

In America

Back in America, English colonists soon learned that the Pequots did not make good slaves. They were too independent, the colonists said, and not easily governed. The Pequots wanted to keep their own religion and way of life. Many Pequots in Massachusetts and Connecticut managed to escape and return to their own people. Those who were caught trying to escape were brought back and **branded** on the shoulder with a hot iron.

Other tribes joined
the English in their
efforts to wipe out
the Pequots.

Chapter Four

A Tribe Divided

The English wanted to get rid of the Pequots altogether. On September 21, 1638 they forced the tribe to sign a treaty forbidding them to return to their old territory. The English also tried to prevent the tribe from reuniting. They divided what was left of the Pequot land between the Narragansetts and the Mohegans. Thus, the Pequots who survived the war were now slaves of the English or under the control of two other tribes.

The Mohegans

The Mohegans are often confused with the Mahicans, who lived in the Hudson River Valley of New York. The Mohegans are also confused with the Mohicans, a **fictional** tribe in James Fenimore Cooper's book *The Last of the Mohicans.* In the early 1600s, the Mohegans split off from the Pequots. When war broke out with English colonists, the Mohegans fought on the English side.

Uncas, the Mohegan sachem, fought the Mohawks. He helped English settlers in Connecticut survive, and they named a town Uncasville after him. A monument in his honor was erected in Norwich, Connecticut. Another stands on the site of James Fenimore Cooper's home in Cooperstown, New York, because Uncas is the name of a character in the author's book.

Historians believe that the word *Pequot* means "people of the shallow waters" in the Algonquian family of languages, to which the Pequot language belongs. But the English said *Pequot* meant "the destroyers" and insisted that the name no longer be used. Still, the Pequots managed to keep their own identity. Those under Mohegan control were now called the Western Pequots. Those under Narragansett control were called the Eastern Pequots.

Two years later, trouble arose between the English and the Narragansetts. The English were afraid the Eastern Pequots would fight alongside the Narragansetts if war broke out, so the English allowed the Eastern Pequots to leave the Narragansetts. With Harmon Garett as their sachem, the Eastern Pequots settled on the coast near the Paucatuck River, which runs along the Rhode Island border into Long Island Sound.

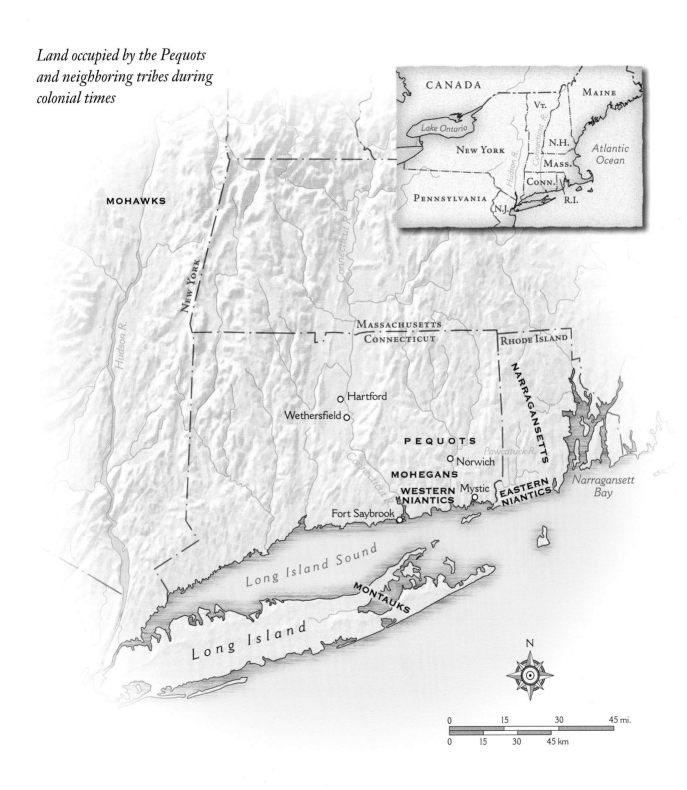

*Land occupied by the Pequots
and neighboring tribes during
colonial times*

CANADA

MAINE

Vt.

Lake Ontario

NEW YORK

N.H.

Connecticut R.

Hudson R.

MASS.

Atlantic
Ocean

CONN.

PENNSYLVANIA

R.I.

N.J.

MOHAWKS

Connecticut R.

New York

Hudson R.

MASSACHUSETTS
CONNECTICUT

RHODE ISLAND

NARRAGANSETTS

Hartford

Wethersfield

PEQUOTS

Pawcatuck R.

Norwich

MOHEGANS

WESTERN
NIANTICS

Mystic

EASTERN
NIANTICS

Narragansett
Bay

Connecticut R.

Fort Saybrook

Long Island Sound

MONTAUKS

Long Island

N

0   15   30   45 mi.

0   15   30   45 km

The Connecticut coast remained home to surviving Pequots.

They became known as the Paucatuck Pequots. In 1661, English settlers drove them across the river into Stonington.

Around the same time, Connecticut's Governor Winthrop allowed the Western Pequots to return to their old territory near the coast. Robin Cassasinamon, who had been a servant of the governor's brother, became their sachem. Cassasinamon brought his people together and remained sachem until his death in 1682. During his term, the Pequots adopted the fox as their **totem,** and began to call themselves the Fox People.

As time passed, more English colonists settled in Connecticut. At first, the new settlers did not infringe on their territory, so the settlers and the Pequots got along well. Colonial

Fox People

The Pequots called themselves the Fox People to honor the many red foxes in their region. The red fox is an excellent hunter, with a keen sense of smell and sharp eyesight.

records show that the Pequots provided the colonists with food and shelter to help them survive their first difficult year. Trouble began when more and more settlers poured into the area. They destroyed Pequot corn, cut down Pequot apple trees, and allowed their animals to graze on Pequot land. Some settlers even built their houses and fences on Pequot land, and some planted crops in Pequot hunting grounds.

Reservation Life

The colonial government kept dividing up the land. Each time it was divided, the colonists got more and the Pequots got less. Even so, settlers continued to behave as if all the land was rightfully theirs. To solve the problem, the colonial government forced both Pequot groups to move 10 miles (16 km) north to one of two **reservations**. This didn't work out, either. Before the war, some Indian chiefs had sold pieces of that land to the ancestors of the new settlers, and the settlers now claimed it was theirs. In exchange for their homes, the Pequots had to work for the settlers.

Arguments arose and the English appointed white overseers to settle them. The overseers usually sided with the settlers and tried to convince the Pequots to live like whites. They banned Schemitzun and other religious rituals, and they tried to convince the Pequots to become Christian and pray

The Feast of the Green Corn and Dance, recreated for today's museum visitors.

quietly inside churches like the English. They didn't under-
stand Indian religions and thought that shamans were in
league with the devil because they prayed outside, moved
about, and sometimes sang loudly.

Population Decline

The Pequot population in Connecticut decreased as fast as the
size of their land did. Many Pequot men were killed in the
French and Indian War (1754–1763), a war fought between
the English and French (with Indian allies on both sides) over
North American territory. By 1762, there were just 176
Pequots left and only twenty or thirty families lived on each

*The French and Indian
War further divided
and weakened the
Pequot nation.*

reservation. Some Pequot men fought in the Revolutionary War (1775–1783), and some spent months at sea on whaling ships when the war ended. Others also left the reservations to find work elsewhere, or joined the Brotherton Movement, a group of displaced members of various eastern tribes led by a Christian missionary. At first, the Brothertons lived in New York State. Later, they moved to Wisconsin and farmed near Lake Winnebago. When whites wanted their land, the Brothertons were forced to move farther north or to Indian Territory (now Oklahoma).

Like her ancestors, this Pequot woman works a small plot of land to help earn her family's living.

Through the years, conditions on both Pequot reservations grew even worse. By 1850, most Pequots had moved away to work in factories, on farms or ships, or as servants in white people's homes. Only about fifty Pequots lived on each reservation, most of them women. They tended the crops, raised their families, picked and sold berries, and sold handmade baskets, wooden bowls, and utensils. They also met in council and handled tribal affairs. After 1900, their main source of income declined because the best basket makers had died. There was little change in either Pequot community for the first forty years of the twentieth century.

Two Tribes

In the 1930s, Atwood Williams, or Chief Silver Star, a Pequot who had lived on both reservations, acted as spokesman for both groups. Williams went to court to object when non-Pequot people moved onto either reservation.

Chief Silver Star also visited local schools to explain Indian heritage to the students. Later, he passed the leadership of the Mashantucket Pequots on to his son-in-law, John George.

By 1940, only two families lived on the Mashantucket reservation. The state had torn down all of the abandoned homes there and would not allow new homes to be built. The Pequots and other tribes in the area formed the American Federation and tried to persuade the state to change its policy, but they did not succeed. Finally, only two elderly sisters remained on Mashantucket. The women scraped out a meager

Tribal Laws

By 1974, the Pequot council had written a constitution for the Mashantucket Tribal Nation. In 1975 Richard Hayward was elected council president.

living by selling berries and handmade baskets. They were determined to stay. They knew that if they left, the state would take over, and the land would no longer belong to the Mashantucket Pequots. Other tribal members and their families met in council in the sisters' home. As a child, Richard Hayward, one of the sisters' grandson, listened when the council discussed the tribe's history and its problems. As Richard grew up, he dreamed of reuniting his people on their rightful land.

Tribal members sold corn and vegetables. They tapped maple trees and boiled the sap to make maple syrup and sold it. They raised chickens and pigs and sold eggs and meat. They cut down trees, and chopped and sold firewood. They dug sand and gravel and washed, sorted, and sold it. They opened a restaurant. For their businesses to succeed, however, they needed money to expand them. The local banks wouldn't lend them any, and their businesses did not earn enough money to support the tribe.

Richard Hayward still dreamed of reuniting the Mashantucket Pequots on their ancestral land. Tribal members wanted the government to provide money for improvements, but first they needed to get federal recognition. They had to prove that the Pequots had always been a tribe. Hayward had archaeologists search for things that showed where the Pequots had lived in the past. "We knew there had to be a story underneath the ground that hadn't been told," said his sister, Theresa H. Bell. She was right. The archaeologists

found pieces of a fortified Pequot village, probably built in 1670, as well as several houses from the 1700s. They dug up wampum, nuts, **flint,** and what may be the oldest peach pit in the Northeast. The archaeologists pieced together hundreds of fragments and discovered that they formed a large cooking pot. They also found objects that proved the Pequots'

The elders did what chores they could to help the Pequot tribe survive on their land.

Surrounded by items crafted by Indians long ago, this boy gets a sense of Pequot history.

ancestors had lived in the area in prehistoric times, more than ten thousand years ago.

Later some archaeological finds were made by accident. In 1997, a contractor hired to build a parking garage noticed some thin, dark stains when he dug into the earth. They looked like chocolate frosting on a vanilla cake. Archaeologists found that the stains were the remains of houses, probably made of wood, covered with animal skins or soil. The layers of dark and light stains show that a family returned to the place each winter and left in summer.

The archaeologists also found garbage dumps that showed differences between what the Pequots really ate and what European records said the Pequots ate. The Europeans were trying to show their influence on the American Indian's diet. The Pequots did eat some domesticated animals such as pigs, but they still ate mostly fish, nuts and berries, and the meat of animals they hunted, which was cooked outdoors in pits.

"We don't need an archaeological site to learn a lot of this," Ms. Bell said when the discoveries were made. "My grandmother still cooks outside, and I have a fire pit, too. But other people need proof to change the history books."

An Act of Congress restored many acres of tribal land to the Pequots.

Richard Hayward and his sister also consulted with lawyers who searched for—and found—historical documents proving that land had been taken from the Mashantucket Pequots illegally. In 1983, after years of struggle, the government restored the Mashantucket reservation to its original size and provided money for improvements. The Pequots, wherever they might be, were urged to come home.

A dancer in tribal regalia at a festival in Haddam, Connecticut

Chapter Five

Today's Pequots

Today, the Pequots in Connecticut are still split into two groups. There are 517 Mashantucket Pequots and 128 Paucatuck Pequots. Half of the Paucatuck Pequots are descendants of Chief Silver Star, who once headed both tribes.

Only about ten people live on the Paucatuck reservation, however, because it is undeveloped. It needs water, a sewer system, and other modern improvements. The Paucatucks cannot afford to clear the land and make the necessary improvements themselves. They are now trying to get federal recognition so that they will be able to get funds to make their reservation a healthy place to live. The Mashantucket Pequots agree that the Paucatucks should get federal recognition.

Bermudans

Descendants of Pequot people who were sold into slavery in Bermuda are still there. Some are sailors or fishermen or ships' pilots. The pilots guide huge ocean liners safely through the same jagged reefs that kept their ancestors prisoner. Some Bermudan Pequots are boat builders, known for their fine craftsmanship. Most have married non-Indians over the years and have been cut off from their Indian heritage for so long that they know little about it. Its influence, however, may still be seen in the routines and costumes of the Bermudan Gombeys. The Gombeys are dancers who have been performing on Bermuda's lanes and streets ever since slavery days. They wear masks and feathered headdresses and often carry tomahawks and bows and arrows. During the dance, a dancer called the Leading Indian sometimes dances well ahead of the other dancers, making a mark on the doorsteps of people who wish to watch them.

By 1994, tribal membership had grown to three hundred. Today, on the Mashantucket reservation, the Pequots have built a casino, a resort, and several other businesses. These provide money for day-care centers, education, and health programs, police and fire departments, and tribal courts. Thousands of Native Americans and other Americans are employed by the Mashantucket Pequots, and they make generous contributions to charities and cultural activities, such as the Special Olympics and the ballet.

Gombey dancers in Bermuda wear feathers and carry tomahawks, reflecting their American Indian roots.

The entrance to the Foxwoods Resort Casino, on the Mashantucket Pequot reservation in southeastern Connecticut

Today's Pequot children hear about the two mythical women who became their tribe's foremothers and the two real women who inspired their tribal nation's remarkable rebirth. However, much Pequot culture—its language, customs, and art—has been lost because the tribe has been scattered for so long. In their careful research, the Pequots collected first hand accounts from the original writings of explorers and preachers.

Tradition Reborn

Today's most important celebration is still Schemitzun, the Feast of the Green Corn and Dance, just as it was before the English banned it. Pequots share the celebration with many other tribes. "It has become known as the granddaddy of all powwows," said Dale Roberts, a Choctaw, who came to Connecticut all the way from Alberta, Canada. He met his parents, who came from Ada, Oklahoma, and the whole family camped out in a pasture near Schemitzun's five-thousand-seat dancing tent.

Ron James Whitewolf, a member of the northern Cheyenne, could not find a dictionary of his tribe's language or a picture of its totem until he found both in the Mashantuckets' extensive library. A leader of the Pueblo people of New Mexico who was visiting the library said the Pueblos will also be coming to research their tribe there.

They also consulted historical maps and reservation records. A new $193 million museum, library, and research center in Mashantucket is helping to restore Pequot and other Native American cultures and preserve their true histories.

At the annual powwow, dancers gather to celebrate their heritage.

The new museum has attracted American Indians belonging to more than five hundred tribal nations in North America. Visitors include dancers, singers, storytellers, professors, and students of American history. Mashantucket is now the American Indians' foremost gathering place.

Timeline of Pequot History

1614	Adriaen Block, a Dutch sea captain, sails into the Pequot region.
1630	Regular contact starts between the Dutch and the Pequots. Trade with the English begins.
1637	War with the English. The main Pequot village is destroyed.
1639	Treaty ends Pequot War with the English. Prisoners of war are enslaved.
1641	The rest of the tribe is divided among other tribes.
1654	Mashantucket Pequots are granted land at Noank, which is now New London.
1666	Noank land is unproductive. The English grant the Mashantucket Pequots additional land near what is now Ledyard.
1683	Paucatuck Pequots are given a reservation in present-day Stonington.
1721	Mashantucket Pequots complete their removal to land near Ledyard.
1770s	Some Pequots join Brotherton Movement and move to New York State.
1860	Both Pequot tribes are reduced to fifty members each.
1901	Fewer than twenty Pequots live on each reservation.
1970s	Elizabeth George Plouffe and Martha Ellal, the last two residents on Mashantucket reservation, die.
1974	The Mashantucket Council completes a constitution for the Mashantucket Pequot Tribal Nation.
1976	Richard Hayward is elected council president.
1998	Mashantucket Pequot Museum and Research Center opens.

Glossary

bounty—reward

branded—marked by burning with a hot iron to show owner-ship

breechcloth—cloth or animal skins that hang from the waist

cormorant—large seabird related to the pelican

fictional—imaginary; made-up

flint—stone that sparks and is used to start fires

immune—protected from infection by previous exposure

porridge—cooked cereal

quahog—a large clam with a hard shell

racist—prejudiced, believing one race is better than another

ransom—money that is demanded for the release of a captive

reservation—an area of land set aside by the government for a special purpose

sachem—leader or chief

sagamore—sachem's assistant

shaman—religious leader

till—to prepare land for planting

totem—a sign or symbol

wampum—tiny beads used to decorate belts and necklaces

wigwam—a hut made of poles and covered with bark or animal skins

To Find Out More

Books

Bruchac, Joseph. *Return of the Sun, Native American Tales from the Northeast Woodlands*. Trumansburg, New York: Crossing Press, 1989.

French and Indian War (World History Series). San Diego, CA: Lucent Books, 1994.

Greene, Jacqueline D. *Powwow*. Danbury, CT: Franklin Watts, 1998.

Marsh, Carole. *Connecticut Indian Dictionary for Kids*. Peachtee City, GA: Gallopade Publishing Group, 1996.

Miller, Jay. *American Indian Foods*. Danbury, CT: Children's Press, 1996.

Ortiz, Simon. *The People Shall Continue*. San Francisco: Children's Book Press, 1988.

Quiri, Patricia Ryon. *The Algonquians*. Danbury, CT: Franklin Watts, 1992.

Sewall, Marcia. *People of the Breaking Day*. New York: Atheneum, 1990.

Organizations and Online Sites

The Gombeys
http://cyberfair.gsn.org/gprep/gombey.html
A brief history of the colorful dancers and how they celebrate holidays such as Boxing Day (December 26) and New Year's Day.

A Man Named Lion
http://www.lihistory.com/3/hs307a.htm
The story of Englishman Lion Gardiner—adventurer, engineer, Connecticut settler, and protestor against the Pequot War.

Mashantucket Pequot Museum and Research Center
http://www.mashantucket.com
Historical information, and details about the Mashantucket Pequot Museum and Research Center.

Powwow

http://www.pride–net.com/native_indians/pow-wow.html
Explains powwow etiquette, terms used, the drum, the dance area, songs and dances, food usually served, and more.

A Note on Sources

I was introduced to the Pequots on a trip to Connecticut where a densely wooded area suddenly opened up, and a scene resembling Oz came into view. It turned out to be The Foxwoods, the Mashantucket Pequots' resort and gambling casino. Curiosity, not gambling, led me inside. In the middle of the spacious lobby was a huge transparent sculpture of an American Indian, his bow and arrow pointed to the sky. In an out-of-the way corner of the casino was a small display, with a bark-covered roundhouse and a brochure with a few brief historical facts. My appetite for more information whetted, I visited my local libraries.

Through several interlibrary loans, hours of browsing through bookstores, and writing letters, I collected my sources. The *Pequots in Southern New England, The Fall and Rise of an American Indian Nation*, edited by Hauptman and Wherry, published by University of Oklahoma Press in 1990, and *The Invasion of America* by Francis Jennings, published by the University of North Carolina Press in 1975, were helpful. So were *History of Indians of Connecticut, from Earliest Known Period to 1850*, published in Hartford in 1852, several encyclopedias on American Indians, old and recent, a detailed history sent to me by the Paucatuck Pequots, and the bibliography sent to me by the Mashantucket librarian, Helene Tieger. For information on the Pequot enslavement in Bermuda, I consulted a dissertation written by Ethel Boissevain, and various issues of the Harvard Alumni Bulletin.

Index

Numbers in *italics* indicate illustrations.

About the Author

Shirlee Petkin Newman has written seventeen books for children, including three for the Franklin Watts Indians of the Americas Series: *The Incas*, *The Inuits*, and *The Creek*. She is currently working on the *The Slave Trade, Slavery in the Americas, and Slavery Today* for the forthcoming Watts Library History of Slavery Series. Her other published books include several biographies, a picture book, three books of fiction, and two collections of folk tales. She has been an Associate Editor at *Child Life* Magazine and has taught courses in *Writing for Children* at Brandeis University, Boston Center for Adult Education, and Cambridge Adult Education Center.